TITLE THEFT QUICK GUIDE of Lists

Investigate!

Evidence you Need
Where to Find It

ALEXANDRA CLAIR

The scanning, uploading, and distribution of this booklet without permission is a theft of the authors intellectual property. Alexandra Clair, d.b.a., Diamond Hedge Productions, LLC.

Copyright: January 2021 / Title Theft Quick Guide of Lists
Registration Number: 2233459
All Rights Reserved

ISBN: 978-0-9847059-7-9

If interested in booking the author as a speaker or for a zoom consultation: (901) 504-9704

Illegal Foreclosure, Title Theft, and its Chain of Corruption | Facebook
https://www.amazon.com/Alexandra-Clair/e/B008PY1XIQ?ref=dbs_a_mng_rwt_scns_share

www.alexandraclair.com

Other Books by, Alexandra Clair
Illegal Foreclosure, Title Theft, and its Chain of Corruption
Wood's End (fiction) Book and Screenplay
The Year Between the Wood (fiction)
Clachan Maze (fiction)
Discerning Spirits: Visionary Gifts in Practice (nonfiction)
"Patrick" Exorcist, Evangelist, Prophet (screen play)

For I the Lord, love justice. I hate robbery and wrongdoing…
(Isaiah 61: 8a).

CONTENTS

DESCRIPTION OF TERMS v

CHAPTER ONE: Use of this Booklet 1

CHAPTER TWO: Variations on Title Theft 3

CHAPTER THREE: Theft Time Line of Events 7

CHAPTER FOUR: Enterprise Plus Relationship 14

CHAPTER FIVE: Securitization and the
MERS MIN Number 18

CHAPTER SIX: Bank Fraud 23

CHAPTER SEVEN: The Mortgage Servicer
Fraud Partner 25

CHAPTER EIGHT: Document Fraud 29

CHAPTER NINE: Closing Agent 32

CHAPTER TEN: HUD assigned Number
Identifiers 34

CHAPTER ELEVEN: The Fraud Narrative 37

CHAPTER TWELVE: Laundering the Digital
Property Title 41

CHAPTER THIRTEEN: Lack of Disclosure is
Strategic and Deliberate 47

CHAPTER FOURTEEN: Title Theft is an Identity Theft Crime 48

CHAPTER FIFTEEN: Fraud Partner – Substitute Trustee 55

CHAPTER SIXTEEN: Instruments of Attack 58

CHAPTER SEVENTEEN: Confusion 63

CHAPTER EIGHTEEN: Notary Fraud 65

CHAPTER NINETEEN: Create a Visual 67

CHAPTER TWENTY: The Perp Wall 70

CHAPTER TWENTY-ONE: Prove What You Say 74

CHAPTER TWENTY-TWO: Okay to be a Nag............ 76

CHAPTER TWENTY-THREE: There are Laws 77

CHAPTER TWENTY-FOUR: Dress Up and Show Up. 80

CHAPTER TWENTY-FIVE: Fraud is the Fly in the Ointment... 82

CHAPTER TWENTY-SIX: CONCLUSION 84

DESCRIPTION OF TERMS

Definition of legal terms can be found in Black's Law Dictionary.
Begin by reading these descriptions. When first appearing in the following chapters these terms will appear in bold text. If need be, go back and reference these descriptions.

Appraisal Fraud: Features heavily in all Property Flip – Title Theft Schemes. Lenders are liable when they fail to confirm valuation(s). When they fail to investigate incomplete and vague reporting. In title theft homes may be undervalued or overvalued.

Asset Manager: This title is used very loosely in mortgage fraud and title theft schemes. The term may apply to the broker that is pooling stolen property titles into a security instrument. It may be used to hide the Perpetrator Nexus money manager identity or that of a realtor or broker flipping stolen property. The title may be assigned to a family member as a ploy to conceal the perpetrator identity. Where this title appears investigate the context and intent of how and why it appears. Always ask: who is the Asset Manager? How is this role worked into the chain of theft? Are they even a real person or entity?

Bank Fraud: Flows two ways. Per criminals perpetrating a fraud upon the bank and when banks allow themselves to be used for illegal purposes. Examples include the following. Theft of money or assets acquired from financial institutions by illegal means. False statements, misrepresentations of value, stolen property titles used as collateral. Banks are liable when they rubber stamp identity theft by failing to take a, hard look at common identity theft breeder documents including the Title Insurance claims. When they fail to report fraud, fail to file Suspicious Activity Reports (SAR), fail to apply uniform fraud detection screening procedures. When they launder income derived from title theft, deed transfers, and mortgage scams. Or when they sell securities backed by Deeds of Trust acquired by robbery to their investor-depositors.

Bank Secrecy Act: (BSA) 31 U.S.C. 5311; U.S. Legislation serving to prevent criminals from using financial institutions to hide or launder money. In a title theft context, the stolen Property Titles are laundered. Funds coming out of these schemes such as house payments styled as Assignment of Rents are laundered. The Bank Secrecy Act establishes reporting and record keeping requirements as well as provisions under the USA Patriot Act: *"for national banks, federal savings associations, federal branches and agencies of foreign banks."* Office of the Comptroller of the Currency (OCC). Deeds of Trust appearing as *document fraud security instruments* as well as dirty money generated from these schemes are laundered in violation of the Bank Secrecy Act. Banks are required to report these crimes. When they fail to do so, they are liable. The reporting threshold is SUSPICION, not proof.

Breeder Document: These are identification documents used to establish phony authority over mortgages and Deeds of Trust. They fuel the document fraud, featured heavily in all Title Theft property flip schemes. Breeder documents displace the real ownership claims seated in the Property Title with that of the robber. Identity theft breeder documents fuel production of security instruments (endorsements) such as the Trustee's Deed of Trust. Breeder documents in the form of document fraud drives the chain of theft obliterating and suppressing the real ownership claims.

Bribe: A bribe is not always about money. It can be the promise of future benefits. It can be the exchange of gifts and services where the bill never comes. It may be disguised as progress that disenfranchise the poor from any ability to fight back. It may even be about black mail and criminal coercion. For how bribes fit into a title theft context, building the criminal enterprise operations, read my book: *Illegal Foreclosure, Title Theft, and its Chain of Corruption;* found on the Alexandra Clair Amazon Author Page.

Broken Chain of Title: Is a feature of all title theft schemes. Missing signed and notarized sales, transfers of authority, Assignment(s) of the Deed of Trust, and "flips" of the Property Title amongst the fraudsters, even family members are concealed and, or, withheld from public access. See: **Chain of Title.** See: **Property Title.** See: **MERSCorp Holdings, Inc.**

Chain of Title: Refers to the unbroken and transparent ownership history of real estate also known as string of title or line of title. Fraud perfecting endorsements, transfers, sales and flips are withheld from public filing, delayed from filing, or blatantly concealed in the bank created MERSCorp Holdings, Inc., E-Registry System. Hiding and concealing select pieces of the title history serve to disenfranchise victims from fighting back. Outcome is **broken chain of title** as a needed fraud-perfecting step of any title theft or mortgage scam and thus, a crime. Title companies are also liable when they withhold some filings, but selectively file others so as to limit disclosure, protect the client, and disguise theft.

Criminal Enterprise: Those persons and services that function together to perfect robbery, identity theft, document fraud, bank fraud and other crimes. *It shall be unlawful for any person employed by or associated with any enterprise engaged in, or the activities of which affect, interstate or foreign commerce, to conduct or participate, directly or indirectly, in the conduct of such enterprise affairs through a pattern of racketeering activity or collection of unlawful debt. RICO: 18 U.S.C. § 1962 /* Worth reading since as they say, "it takes a village." Title theft operates within a local and national footprint.

Digital Property Title: Assumption of the electronic property title is the precursor to illegal seizure of the physical premises. The digital property title is electronically laundered as the fraudsters bury the Deed of Trust and Property Title in your name under the weight of document fraud. Robbery does NOT start with illegal seizure. It starts when criminals, working behind the scenes take control of the electronic title to your home and begin laundering the Property Title via secret transfers, assigns, sales, and loans. Each secret transaction, in whatever form that takes, serve to quash your rights, while building the identity theft claims of ownership over property titles acquired by robbery.

Document Fraud: Features and drives all title theft schemes. The criminal Note-Holder/Note-Owner names hide behind obscure terms or other identifiers like that of your former lender, a shell company, a defunct company or MERS. Every false statement and example of forgery render those documents null and void with no power to enforce. Document fraud appears as notary stamps and signatures lifted from other documents, robosigned security instruments, phony or altered names and dates, fictitious claims of value, etc. Document fraud moves the theft trajectory toward the goal of illegal seizure in violation of the Fourth Amendment to the U.S. Constitution, **"under color of law."**

Endorsements: Signed and notarized security instruments that sell, transfer, or assign theft perfecting authority to fraud partners. The endorsement is affirmed by signatures and, or, by notary stamp and signature. Parties sign and covenant that what is stated within is true; absent all fraud, forgery, doubt, and error. Courts have ruled that these signed and notarized instruments carry the weight of a contract. When any part is not true all assignments, transfers, sales subsequent to and pertinent to, falsifications within, render trailing documentation unenforceable; null and void. See: **Property Title; See Chain of Title.**

Enterprise plus Relationship: Each individual person, company, or entity that played a part in moving the chain of theft forward is part of the "perpetrator nexus" or, in a RICO context, they are part of the criminal enterprise. *"A sufficient nexus or relationship exists between the racketeering acts and the enterprise if the defendant was able to commit the predicate acts by means of, by consequences of, by reason of, by agency of, or by instrumentality of his association with the enterprise." Marino vs. ME Department of Corrections; First Circuit Court of Appeals.*

Fraud Narrative: This is the rationale for how and why you lost your home. In fact, your home is not something you misplaced. Your home was stolen per a, very specific chain of theft. The fraud narrative infects official records. It then plays out in how the chain of theft is structured and fitted to your individual circumstances. Disclosures that you are legally entitled to are systematically withheld at every juncture where you might be enabled to fight back. The lies appear **"under color of law"** at the start of the chain of theft. This "story" is carried forward as a thread to infect by slander other documents repeating so often that it is thought no one will believe you. See: **Document Fraud.**

Grantee: The person or entity receiving the property by conveyance of an endorsement; signed and notarized paper or written agreement.

Grantor: The person or entity granting the property to the Grantee.

Identity Theft: Via use of breeder documents the homeowner identity is supplanted by that of the secret Note-Holder/Note-Owner. A title theft property flip scheme is a form of identity theft and also a RICO Predicate Act. The digital property title cannot be controlled until the identity theft piece, supported by the fraud narrative is established in multiple records. When looking for an attorney find one that specializes in bringing identity theft claims against perpetrators; recovering assets for victims. Steer clear of attorneys that make a living defending the perpetrators since they may be more likely, for favor or a payout, to dumb down your case.

Illegal Foreclosure, Title Theft, and its Chain of Corruption; April 2020. This book provides more detail about the Bank Theft Delivery System. How America's banks are stealing homes, pooling them into securities and feeding stolen property as price fixed rentals to the securities market. Variations on Title Theft are described. I share my own personal story and the corruption I experienced at every turn. https://www.amazon.com/Alexandra-Clair/e/B008PY1XIQ%3Fref=dbs_a_mng_rwt_scns_share

Interim Period: This middle period is lucrative for the white-collar criminals. This is the period that the property title is slandered, laundered, and equity is skimmed. Laundering the chain of property title during this interim period takes place absent all legally required disclosure coming to homeowner-targets of these schemes. Title theft is fueled by the abject failures of banks, title insurance companies, and other entities to apply fundamental levels of due diligence. As set up for the illegal seizures this is the period that the mortgage is driven into default and the identity theft claims over the property title are established.

Laundering the Chain of Property Title: Distance must exist between your Property Title or Deed of Trust and the identity theft claims over homes acquired by robbery. This occurs by document fraud. The digital property title is secretly laundered via various transfers, sales, and assignments of authority amongst fraud partners. Each secret transaction going unchallenged establishes the identity theft claims of the criminal while suppressing and quashing the homeowner claims. Acquiring your mortgage, driving it into default, laundering the electronic property title with no meaningful disclosure to you, positioning you as helpless to fight back as the chain of theft unfolds violate the *Truth in Lending Act of 1968*. Make a study of this very important federal law.

Mail and Wire Fraud: Are featured in all title theft and mortgage theft schemes. Involves mailing or electronically transmitting contracts, security instruments, funds, or instructions amongst fraud partners and enablers. Gather the for-hire contracts at the discovery phase or, if possible, before. Never give up asking for what you need. A few low-level employees may send you what the company itself, concealing fraud, would never send. A mail clearing center is often hired to control the flow of information. An extortionist debt collector is often hired. A Title Insurance company is hired. These schemes' often use the letterhead of other parties like your original lender or bank. This serves to disguise the identity of the secret Note-Holder/Note-Owner driving forward the chain of theft. Mail and Wire Fraud are RICO Predicate Acts; 18 U.S.C. 1961.

MERSCorp Holdings, Inc.; (MERS) is a shell company created by the financial services industry. They function in part to replace and undermine the integrity of the public land records and in particular the Registrar of Deeds Office. Versions of the MERS name may appear as the proxy identity used to disenfranchise homeowners from any recognition of the true Note-Holder/Note-Owner criminal identity driving the digital property title toward the goal of illegal seizure. MERSCorp Holdings, Inc., also known as Mortgage Electronic Registration System or the MERS E-Registry System function as the data base depository for title theft as an identity theft crime. Missing sales, assignments and transfers that launder the chain of title, while skimming equity are withheld from the Registrar of Deeds Office and concealed in the MERS System. Chapter Nineteen of my book: *Illegal Foreclosure, Title Theft, and its Chain of Corruption* is entirely devoted to MERS. This chapter should be read by every citizen investigator. It should be read by those that want to restore and reform the public land recordation system to its former levels of trust. Lost filing fees in the millions of dollars are captured by MERS and lost to county budgets.

Mortgage Fraud: If the home being targeted for title theft carries a mortgage that mortgage must be driven into default. This starts with the fraud narrative intruding into financial records. It requires a third-party mortgage servicer company having trained their employees in the bullying art of misrepresentations of authority and harassment. These companies will often masquerade as the original lender or bank to thus, conceal the secret Note-Owner or Note-Holder criminal identity. Get the for-hire contract. Save all mail that may be coming on letterhead of the original lender.

The NEMO DAT RULE: A common-sense fairness principal that most of us learned on the playground as children. *Nemo Dat Quod Non Habet; "no one gives what he does not have."* This principal under law states that the purchase of a possession from someone who had no rightful ownership claim will in turn deny that purchaser any rightful ownership title or claim to that property. In other words, where title theft or mortgage fraud has taken place you still own your home. There is no statute of limitations on a void judgement. Read up on Void Judgements.

Procedural Due Process: This is the legal doctrine in the United States that requires government officials (and those entities chartered under federal law) to follow fair procedures before depriving a person of life, liberty, or property. Think outside the box.

Property Flip Scheme: In complex title theft schemes the stolen property title has to be laundered. Thus, there will be multiple behind the scenes transactions and transfers of the property title orchestrated by and taking place amongst the white-collar criminals. Every flip of the digital property title (start, middle, end) comprises the big picture chain of theft.

Property Title: Refers to who has legal ownership and the right to use of land, dwellings and buildings situated on that land. The ownership rights must be proven via an unbroken document trail of notarized paper that is traceable through the endorsement of those that sign these documents. See: **Chain of Title.**

REO Investors: Are persons or groups that invest in at risk mortgages and bank owned property. Every parasite needs a host. Some of these homes end up pooled with other homes into security instruments marketed to the unwitting public. When legitimate foreclosures could not keep up with demand for securities backed by deeds of ownership the Bank Theft Delivery System was conceived. This system, uses "insider" approved bank vendors. The bank vendor system is used by the criminal REO Investors who act as the boots on the ground local arm of operations; profiling and targeting homeowners as unlikely to fight back. The chain of theft operates within a local and a national footprint making up the mafia like criminal operations and thus, qualifies as a RICO Criminal Enterprise. **The Bank Theft Delivery System** is detailed in my book: *Illegal Foreclosure, Title Theft, and its Chain of Corruption.*

Robo-Judge: The robo-judge is predisposed for whatever reason to rubber stamp the claims of the foreclosing parties. They resist any continuance that may allow you time to investigate title theft or mortgage fraud. They will fail to enforce disclosure of a full chain of property title including the complete <u>MERSCorp Holdings</u> transaction (flipping) history. They allow attorneys to speak for perpetrator-clients that never appear in the flesh and in fact are not accurately identified. They may oppose the concept that Title Theft is an identity theft scheme. They may be personally invested in securities backed by price fixed rentals and may have conflicts of interest with those that commit these crimes. Where the appearance of and, or, even the possibility of any conflict of interest exists, it is your right to ask for a new judge. If any judge limits your ability to defend your interests quote the U.S. Supreme Court ruling in Caperton vs A.T. Massey Coal Company; 556 U.S. 868 (2009). This now famous ruling held that the Due Process Clause of the Fourteenth Amendment requires a judge to recuse themselves even when there is the "probability of bias." Do not be the sitting duck these suits expect you to be.

Robosigners: As described by the Department of Housing and Urban Development (HUD). *"We have defined the term "robosigning" as the practice of an employee or agent of the servicer signing documents automatically without a due diligence review or verification of the facts."*

Securitization / Mortgage-Backed Securities: This is the practice of pooling residential mortgages into security instruments that are then bought and sold over the secondary markets many times over. These poorly regulated practices have fueled theft of American homes.

Shell Company: A shell company owns nothing. In our context they operate to conceal the arm-in-arm chain of theft, source of dirty money, and recognition of the perpetrator(s) identity. Title theft operatives hide behind shell companies and other proxy identifiers.

Source Document(s): The Deed of Trust, Promissory Note, or whatever documents exists by which the home was purchased and, or, deeded to you at the time of purchase. The title theft time line begins with slandering and thus, corrupting the authority of the Source Document(s). Per the identity theft step-process the perpetrator(s) must replace your ownership rights with that of theirs and, or, with that of a straw buyer. See: **Fraud Narrative**

Straw Buyer: Straw buyers are used to conceal the actual Note-Holder/Note-Owner criminal identity. Use of straw buyers feature heavily in title theft schemes. They may be a family member, a phony identity, an alias, or the person that, while claiming to be the new owner is in fact a renter, renting the property for a limited period of time. The straw buyer identity may later appear as the selling party noted within MLS Listings. They may appear as the party that flips the property back to the REO Investors by Quit Claim Deed or Warranty Deed only when it is considered safe to do so. When looking at the chain of title, do background checks on names that appear. Tie straw buyers to the criminal enterprise operations. In title theft, on the face of those filings, endorsements, and instruments what may appear to be legitimate, is actually a clever façade, more lies, and other examples of document fraud.

Substitute Trustee: A new trustee is appointed willing to preside over the illegal flip or transfer of property titles acquired by robbery back to the criminal enterprise. The valid role of any trustee must take authority from a clean and unbroken chain of Property Title free of fraud, doubt, errors, and forgery. Where title theft crimes are operating there is no clean chain of title. For this reason, the substitute trustee is acting in bad faith. They are orchestrating illegal seizures, under color (cover) of law for their white-collar criminal clients. Tie them to the criminal enterprise operations.

Theft Time Line: That period of time between acquisition and control over the digital property title and, or, the mortgage up to that point in time that the goals of the criminal enterprise are achieved. The theft time-line always extends beyond the illegal seizure. See **Interim Period.** See **Straw Buyer.**

Title Insurance Company: This bank approved vendor will examine the title history to your home and put forth a professional opinion that the property title is free of misrepresentations of authority, fraud, errors, doubt, forgery, and theft. They will then indemnify these claims per an insurance policy taken out by the REO Investors. The role they play is crucial to any title theft or mortgage scam. Title Insurance Companies sell banks on the notion that they will take the hit when fraud is exposed. Name the Title Insurance Company in any lawsuit you file. The title policy itself will vomit up a wealth of information helpful to any lawsuit you file. See: **REO Investors.** See: **Breeder Documents.**

Title Theft Scheme: By illegal and clandestine means the fraudster will create false documents putting forth false claims of ownership. A title theft scheme corrupts the chain of Property Title. Bank fraud will follow as criminal(s) attempt to sell the home or skim equity via loans using the theft asset (your home) as collateral.

Tortious Interference: Features in all title theft schemes. Your Deed of Trust is a contract between you and your lender. Intentional interference with contractual relations causing economic harm is a crime.

Under Color (Cover) **of Law:** Title theft operates as a sequence of crimes under the pretense of being lawful. **Document fraud** is crafted to provide *plausible deniability*. This appearance of something being lawful is used to obstruct recognition of title theft as an identity theft crime operating within the framework of having laundered the chain of property title. Criminals establish the pretense of complying with laws via the instrumentality of document fraud. Interim players and bad actors may be bribed or otherwise induced to obstruct fraud detection screening procedures, due diligence requirements and other safe guards to thus overcome or bypass compliance with state and federal laws, federal regulations, and internal policies and procedures. Asking judges to bypass due process, failing to verify proper notice so as to rubber stamp title theft is: Deprivation of Rights Under Color of Law: 18 U.S.C., 242. Read up on Void Judgements.

CHAPTER ONE
Use of this Booklet

For a quick reference leaf through these pages and find the various lists in this booklet. They serve as a reminder of what you need, keeping your investigation on track as you gather needed proof of title theft and mortgage scams.

Title theft criminals troll for victims. They have gone so far as to recruit spies working in short or long-term care facilities feeding leads into the pipe line of likely victims. Any prolonged absence from the home. Any crisis or personal tragedy that is thought to disable critical thinking skills means that anyone can be a victim.

What drives the selection process deciding what families and what homes get targeted? The answer should alarm every American.

1.) Homes with equity. Real equity the brass ring and therefore many senior citizens, like me, more likely to be targeted. Homes with equity are undervalued per the first appraisal at the start of the Property Flip sequence. This secures the inflated home improvement loans since any brain-dead loan officer can see that the loan is fully collateralized by the theft-asset, aka, your home.

2.) Homes with no equity; mortgages perceived as already in trouble. Every option normally open to those in trouble is blocked. The Property title acquired by fraud, is already secretly vested with the REO Private Investors before the redundant foreclosure charade plays out. Acting as aggressive debt collectors, fraud partners will threaten and coerce house payments with tacked on servicing fees for as long as homeowners can be manipulated to feed the coffers of title theft thieves.

3.) With or without equity any victim profiled as unlikely to fight back. This vulnerability is leveraged. Theft of the **Property Title** takes place within the appalling and illegal absence of disclosures wielded like a weapon by financial industry partners.

CHAPTER TWO
Variations on Title Theft

Title theft can be grouped into two broad categories. When there is a mortgage, more paper is required to perfect the theft. This is a more complex scheme. No mortgage translates to less paper.

If targeted by someone known to the victim this is usually a more simple, concise chain of theft; requiring fewer participants. Every official looking document, greasing the chain of theft can be downloaded from the internet, filled out and usually filed no questions asked, no perjury statement required at the Registrar of Deeds Office in your county.

As your investigation proceeds it will become clear into which title theft picture your experience fits. Stay open to the possibility that multiple aspects of any combination are possible and may apply.

1. **Simple Title Theft:** Committed by a local group of operatives. Even by a greedy family member, acquaintance, or untrustworthy attorney anticipating that at some point in the future they will execute the last wishes of a client. A simple title theft commitment requires fewer examples of document fraud.
2. **Complex Title Theft** is assisted by the Bank Theft Delivery System of approved vendors. Banks off-load securitized mortgages to

criminals and pretend not to know that the sole intent is theft; driving the mortgage into default. This theft commitment requires more paper than would otherwise be necessary. Much of that document fraud is concealed in the bank created **MERSCorp Holdings, Inc.;** MERS E-Registry System; generally referred to as MERS.

3. **Complex Title Theft Schemes may include Securities Fraud.** Homes are backed out of one security and pooled into another. This practice defrauds the former investors as occurred on a massive scale with the former Countrywide CWALT pools of mortgages. The raided and forced divestiture pool of mortgages is forwarded to a broker and will become a reconstituted instrument for investment whose source is robbery. Local REO Private Investors are used as conduits feeding stolen property, acquired via title theft schemes to companies like Pretium Partners, LLC; operating under shell company names in different states. After any illegal seizure has taken place, verify if within the following eighteen months there has been a Quit Claim Deed or a Warranty Deed transfer of your home from a **straw buyer**, or private investor to any corporate entity or shell company.

Fraud partners are styled as locally situated **REO Investors.** These persons or groups are engaged in "rescuing underperforming mortgages" for a profit. They help to shift the debt ratio of banks and are recruited to feed homes to the yawning jaws of the securities industry. These securities are sold to bank investor-depositors returning long term profit back to the financial industry that put this theft pipeline in place.

The intrusion of foreign ownership of American homes and farmland has led to the growth of *absentee landlordism*. Historically this practice has never worked out well. Dismantling private property rights is a socialist agenda leading to homelessness and price fixed rentals. Enemies of this country like China and drug cartels are invested in title theft practices. It stands to reason that bases of operation and safe houses whose property title and ownership history concealed by document fraud and shell companies is just one prong of any agenda to destabilize America from within.

The network of fraud enablers will help to **launder** the **Property Title.** While this is going on you are strategically deprived of all meaningful information that would empower you to fight back. Every flip of the property title, via bank loans and transfers of authority amongst fraud partners going off without any challenge serves to establish an ever-growing gulf of distance between the last filed document at the Registrar of Deeds Office appearing in your name(s) and the criminal claims of ownership.

Most Registrar of Deeds Offices have enabled remote access. You pay a fee and can then download and print to your computer the signed and notarized endorsements on file such as your original Deed of Trust and everything else that follows. This is public information.

Over time I lost track of how much money I spent as I downloaded or paid copying fees. If for some reason you cannot afford to pay these fees contact the Registrar and, or, the Mayor of your county and tell them that you are investigating title theft. You need access to your own personal documents as well as some others at no charge. Ask when the last time it was that any audit of the Registrar of Deeds Office was conducted. Ask for a copy of that audit. No easy access, something to hide.

CHAPTER THREE
Theft Time Line of Events

In more complex title theft schemes, there are six key players to identify. In naming the group of individuals, corporations, banks and other entities' you are able to recognize when the theft started, by what means it proceeded, and when it ended. This is your **Theft Time Line.**

You need everything you can get your hands on falling within the theft time line. The fraud scheme starts when your Deed of Trust, Promissory Note, or owner of record filings as the quintessential **Source Document(s)** are first assumed control over by criminals. This event may be a simple **identity theft** act, filing fictitious ownership records into the public land recordation system. Or it may be more complex. If a mortgage is involved the Bank must off-load control over your mortgage to criminal-partners. They become the new Note-Owner or the new Note-Holder of record. The private investor now has control over the electronic property title and mortgage. This is set up for driving any mortgage into default.

The chain of theft may not end with the illegal seizure. You want to know the destination of where your property title ends up and with whom. If the goal is securities fraud there is almost always a delay before the property title is transferred by Warranty Deed, pooled into a security with other homes, also acquired by robbery per the Bank Theft Delivery System of operation.

At the start of my investigation, I was wrong about almost everything including when my particular theft time line began and when it actually ended. I eventually uncovered five known flips of my property title during the **interim period** that the property title to 65 Pinehurst Drive (Oakland, TN) was laundered. One of these flips was a bank loan for 100k with JP Morgan Chase Bank. Performing no due diligence JP Morgan Chase Bank just handed over 100k of my equity to the REO white-collar scam artists. Proof of this was later found concealed in the **MERSCorp Holdings, inc., MERS E-Registry System**.

Another shock came when I realized that I knew some of the local perpetrator REO group styled as investors. One of these persons, under the pretense of being a good neighbor and friend had been assigned to keep track of how well the wall of deception was holding up during the interim period that, with no disclosure to me, my home was flipped and equity was skimmed. This same strategy was heartlessly repeated with other victims. Be prepared to be surprised by what you uncover. White collar criminals are devious, dangerous, and lacking in conscience.

The date that criminals assume control and authority over the electronic (digital) title to your home is the premier event. This date has to be moved forward in the public records so that you cannot recognize when you were targeted; when the theft actually took place. By design all blame must shift to the homeowner. The **Fraud**

Narrative as the rationale for why you lost your home is secretly established, slandering both you and your **Property Title** during the **Interim Period** that the title is being flipped (laundered). Think of foreclosure and illegal seizure as being entirely redundant and fictitious events existing only to hide when the theft actually took place. To thus, deceive homeowners, heirs, courts, and judges.

There are six key fraud partners. In less complex title theft schemes fewer bad actors will emerge. Take what fits and leave the rest. The key players flesh out the **Criminal Enterprise** operations. For this reason, you need to assign a name to the conduct; identifying the roles that each played.

1. <u>Your Lender</u> who under the contract of your Deed of Trust loaned you money to buy your home; that money secured by the physical premises of your home. Banks knowingly off-load control of the digital property title to criminals who will then drive the mortgage into default. No disclosure to you that a new Note-Holder/Note Owner is calling the shots. From this point forward you have no idea with whom you are communicating, nor the purpose of that deflective and, or, bullying and disrespectful interaction at any given time.

2. <u>Mortgage Electronic Registration System</u>; **MERS Corp Holdings, Inc., the MERS E-Registration System. MERS** is a big player and primary force in the complex globalist agenda to

undermine private property rights in the United States. They conceal within their system fraud perfecting transfers, loans, and assigns of authority by which the stolen Property Titles are laundered. Read any version of the MERS name and until proven otherwise think **Broken Chain of Title**. Think something to hide. Think fraud.

3. Third-party mortgage servicer company(s). They are hired by the secret Note-Holder/Note-Owner as debt collectors. You think they are accepting house payments and servicing your loan. Big mistake! Where fraud is involved, they are hired to string you along and, or, harass you into abandoning your home. Every penny that can be skimmed during the interim period will be skimmed via this partnership. They are not hired to fix disputes. Any change in servicer is a red flag. Find out who hired them. It may be that any new mortgage servicer company is hired to lay the groundwork for the upcoming illegal seizure. For a complete picture of how this works read my book: *Illegal Foreclosure, Title Theft, and its Chain of Corruption*.

4. REO Private Investor Groups. Sometimes called Institutional or Private Investors. Read these names and think fraud until proven otherwise. These white-collar criminals profile victims and target them to the bank that holds the mortgage. The REO Private Investors become the secret Note-Holder/Note-Owner with power to drive the mortgage into default. The end game

returns long-term profit back to the criminal banks. For a complete picture of how this works read my book.

5. <u>The Title Insurance Companies</u> are usually bank approved vendors. They are contracted by the REO Investors for the sole purpose of asserting to lenders that there is a clean, unbroken, and complete chain of property title free of fraud, doubt, error, and forgery. Equity cannot be skimmed and the property title cannot be laundered absent a clean chain of property title. The hire of partners that have credentials the REO Investor Groups may lack are shielded by title insurance companies agreeing to take the hit when bank fraud and title theft is exposed.

6. <u>The foreclosure mill attorneys</u>. Or any attorney acting as a debt collector. Closing any loan or hired to probate a will. Title theft is lawyer heavy. Foreclosure mill attorneys create and file forged, reformed, theft concealing endorsements (signed and notarized instruments) into the public record. They then show up in court to defend the title theft they helped to enable and expect **robo-judges** to rubber stamp. Foreclosure mill attorneys are hired by the REO secret Note-Holders/Note-Owners. They actively conceal the fraudster identities often claiming that the original lender is bringing the foreclosure action.

Foreclosure mill attorneys are full-fledged partners in crime. By tracing the endorsements that they file other victims targeted by the same investor-perpetrators can be identified. This will allow any attorney you hire to establish pattern example statistics.

You will unearth your perpetrator list from those names found within the security instruments and endorsements, MLS listings and other paper.

A superficial reading may appear correct. Facts seem to match up or match the phony bill of good you were sold. Tie the intent of any document to the subsequent next step required of the theft agenda.

Once you dig into your investigation you will find that theft of your home is not hard to recognize. Specific theft goals are accomplished by Document Fraud. This instrumentality drives the chain of theft forward to completion.

1. First, your Deed of Trust is buried under layers of document fraud. Lies and salient omissions of fact render any document null and void.
2. Second, your identity is supplanted by the white-collar criminal claims of ownership. A title theft **property flip scheme** is a form of **Identity Theft**.
3. Third, document fraud is indiscriminately accepted and filed into the Registrar of Deeds Office. You are led to believe you are looking at a complete **Chain of Title**. Nothing could be further from the truth. No one tells you that other secret transactions and transfers of authority are concealed in the MERS System; withheld from public filing. To thus, deliver the needed **Broken Chain of Title.** If at any time you had access

to the complete record, you would recognize the theft timeline. You would uncover the step theft process. You would know who to name in any lawsuit you file. You would be fully equipped to fight back.

The purpose of all this document fraud invites you to give up before you begin. Take the Registrar of Deeds filings in hand. Read them in the order they were filed. Make a cup of tea. Have handy a high-lighter. Make a list of every term you don't understand. Sit in a comfortable chair. If necessary, use a magnifying glass. **Part three of my book: Illegal Foreclosure, Title Theft, and its Chain of Corruption** will take you through the document fraud in other cases, including some lawsuits. At least some of this content will apply to you. There are commonalities in every example of title theft and mortgage fraud. As you identify the common features that surface in every investigation you will feel equipped and empowered to persevere. Knowing the truth will also free you from some of the trauma you've experienced. It will transform helpless pain into righteous indignation fueling your desire for justice and by extension helping others.

CHAPTER FOUR
Enterprise Plus Relationship

Build your perpetrator list. Your perpetrator list and the roles played by each will tell you what variation of the title theft scheme assaulted you and your home.

There is a <u>national footprint of operations</u>. There is the <u>local footprint of operations</u>. These footprints overlap and will flesh out your defendant list in any lawsuit you may decide to file.

The local footprint is seen in the group of local fraudsters often styled as REO Investors. It is exposed via the local services networked or hired by the REO Fraudsters. The national footprint is best seen in the actions of banks and bank approved vendors networked to the local groups of operation.

Each cog in the wheel making title theft possible, comprise the complete criminal enterprise operations. These operational partnerships are known as: **Enterprise plus Relationship.** Enterprise plus relationship is the local footprint of operations tied to the national footprint of operations; individuals and companies. As the big picture these two footprints overlap and work in tandem in what I describe in my book as the Bank Theft Delivery System; (*Illegal Foreclosure, Title Theft and its Chain of Corruption.*)

State laws have not kept up with the growth of title theft. Targeted homeowners are not alerted to potential title theft assaults at multiple junctures where red flags exist. Lots of people fail to do their job and regardless of intent are sucked under the umbrella of the theft perfecting criminal enterprise.

Your perpetrator list will establish, **Enterprise plus Relationship**. There is one chain of theft, but there are multiple parties that by their actions contribute to the enterprise operations. You will endeavor to tie the arm-in-arm services and parties that deliver those services to the goals of the criminal enterprise. "Same" to mean connected and therefore, "part of."

1. Same enterprise broker
2. Same enterprise realtor
3. Same enterprise appraiser
4. Same enterprise straw buyer
5. Same seller – same buyer flipping the property title
6. Same secret Note-Holder/Note-Owner
7. Same closing entity
8. Same loan officer
9. Same underwriter
10. Same enterprise lawyers

Your perpetrator list will grow out of the documents that you gather.

1. Filed at the Registry of Deeds Office in your county.
2. Any closing documents including the HUD-1.
3. All documents filed with MERS.
4. From the REO asset manager(s).

5. Bank Loans including phony home improvement loans.
6. For hire contracts, including that between the third-party mortgage servicer companies and the white-collar scam artists. You are entitled to this disclosure under the Truth in Lending Act.
7. Consider any involvement of Core Logic services suspicious until proven otherwise. In particular use of the Core Logic Equator platform sending and confirming instructions keeping all the fraudsters on the same page. Read my book for more about this.
8. Real estate disclosure forms.
9. What is stated within the Multiple Listing Service (MLS) history of listings both public and those deemed, "not for publication." All photographs found on line tied to any internet listing. Same MLS Number, but different content is a forgery and thus, a fraud device.
10. Any secret, nonpublic, REO website list of properties.
11. Names of that person, trust vehicle, shell company or attorney claiming to pay the property taxes. Everything claimed within the complete Property Tax payment history.
12. Names, including MERS members, emerging from the public record filings. From MERSCorp Holdings, Inc., electronic history of filings.
13. Names and corporate identities coming out of the Title Insurance policies.

14. Names of persons and companies extracted from the HUD-1 closing documents; coughing up a wealth of information. File a FOIA request for every HUD-1 attached to your property address falling within the theft time line you've established. If HUD proves difficult know that here is another government agency self-protecting to conceal corruption within their ranks. Move up the chain of command, write letters, make phone calls, be persistent.
15. Every appraiser. Whether a broker price opinion or any appraiser licensed by the state and by HUD.

CHAPTER FIVE
Securitization and the MERS MIN Number

Before the ink is dry at most home closings the mortgage is securitized as an investment vehicle. The papers you sign allow this. You can decide that you will not allow your mortgage to be securitized into an investment tool, but will require one lender to hold and service your mortgage. If you are then abruptly turned down for a mortgage previously approved up to a set price then by all means file a lawsuit for discrimination as a civil rights violation. Banks and mortgage brokers/lenders operate under a federal charter that disavows discrimination.

Appearing in some filings and not others the MERS MIN Number will tell you what bank initially held your mortgage before control was hijacked by criminals. From start to finish the secret REO Note Holder will continue to hide their identity behind that of MERS, or some other bank tied to your original loan. The fraudsters have access to use of the MERS system helping to conceal their real identity up to and after the charade of foreclosure and illegal seizure. Every bank, the bank servicers, as well as the title insurance companies are MERS Members. They have access to use of the MERS system which functions as the identity theft depository for **Mortgage Fraud** and Title Theft.

Look for and find the MERS MIN Number. The best description of what and how the MERS MIN Number functions comes from: *McDonnell Property Analytics; City of Seattle Review of Mortgage Documents; Appendix "I" Definition of terms.*

MIN Number: The Mortgage Identification Number (MIN) is an 18-digit number that uniquely identifies a mortgage loan registered on the MERS® System. A MIN is permanently assigned to a mortgage at registration and cannot be duplicated or reused.

To process information on the MERS® System, you must enter a MIN. The 18-digit mortgage identification number ("MIN") required for each loan registered on the MERS® System must be placed in a visible location on the cover page (or first page if there is no cover page) of each of the following documents:

(a) *Mortgage or deed of trust,*
(b) *Any other Security Instrument,*
(c) *Assignment of the Security Instrument to or from MERS,*
(d) *Lien release or reconveyance and*
(e) *Any other instrument recorded in the public land records in which MERS has a legal interest.*

The 18-digit MIN Number will show up on the Deed of Trust and on the Assignment of the Deed of Trust. The Assignment of the Deed of Trust is described further along because it functions as one of three key identity theft **Breeder Documents**.

By the time this number shows up on the Assignment of the Deed of Trust, transferring your ownership claims to that of the fraudster, your mortgage no longer exists. It has been hijacked. House payments are captured and styled as assignment of rents in the criminal enterprise year-end IRS filings. No one tells you that per document fraud you are at some point characterized as a renter. If you had any of the information you were lawfully entitled to you would fight back.

Where fraud exists, you may read the original lenders name on letter-head as one of many examples of mail fraud and ongoing deception that keeps you in the dark. Title theft and mortgage schemes by design string you along up to the time that the planned and orchestrated harassment begin with issues and problems you can never fix. This harassment is set up for the illegal seizures. More often than not it begins only after equity is skimmed.

For criminal theft of American homes to operate on a massive scale the Bank Theft Delivery system operating through bank approved vendor-partners do not want to deal with American citizens armed to fight back. The last thing they want is that you can talk about and describe the chain of theft with authority. The corrupt system must hold the line against Fourth Amendment assaults seated in illegal seizures of private property.

It has been my prayer that a whole crop of attorneys will reject criminal defense work and embrace this field on behalf of victims.

Regard use of MERS MIN Number as a potential fraud device until proven others. It may be used to say that the original lender still holds the mortgage when nothing could be further from the truth. The criminals need courts, judges, and especially you to believe that no change of ownership in the form of an REO investor has hijacked the mortgage with no disclosure coming to you. Tell the judge that you suspect title theft and need time to investigate. Ask the judge to issue an order that requires the other side to supply a full and complete list from MERS of every sale, transfer, assign of authority, i.e., the full MERS record tied to your property address, name and mortgage number. As well as any endorsement withheld from filing by the local title company or loan closer. You need a full chain of title. Take every opportunity to ask for this.

If any judge refuses you postponement of any decision allowing you time to investigate Title Theft you have grounds for an appeal.

The MERS layer is recent, has never been needed, and is needed now only to deprive the homeowner of a full and transparent history of how many times their mortgage has shifted through the financial system as a monetary instrument over which homeowners that allow securitization have no control.

After you locate the MIN Number log into the MERS Servicer ID site. Type in the eighteen-digit number. This will tell you what bank/lender originated the mortgage; whether that mortgage is active or inactive. If the Mortgage reads "inactive" but all communication still comes on the letterhead of your original lender something is seriously wrong. Your mortgage has very likely been off-loaded to criminals.

In mortgage fraud and title theft, just for starters there are multiple violations of the Truth in Lending Act. During my investigation it was not unusual to find that there were so many assignments (transfers) and flips of a mortgage that MERS refused to publicly list them all. Get the complete assignment, sale, and transfer history of your mortgage. It is not just that the theft time line will be informed by the MERS filing history, but the complete chain of theft may be laid out in this record that no one wants you to see.

Though too many are slow to this fight, enlist the help of the Registrar of Deeds Official in your county. They should care that the public recordation system is daily more and more corrupted by the MERS dual and secret registry. They should care about all the filing fees lost to their county. In addition, call your state representative. Direct them to this booklet.

CHAPTER SIX
Bank Fraud

In title theft banks routinely walk out the charade of filling out paperwork that postures compliance with a regulation, law, or act of required due diligence absent all the work required to meet those requirements. **Document fraud** is mailed and wired to loan officers, underwriters, loan closers, loan brokers and other recipients. Each is a single example of **Wire Fraud** or **Mail Fraud.** Each time money is skimmed using stolen property as collateral the fraudsters are committing bank fraud.

Bank employees are trained to recognize financial crimes. Employers are responsible when their employees commit crimes. Name any bank that assisted in **laundering your Property Title;** helping to establish the identity theft claims of the robber(s).

Banks are required by law to file a Suspicious Activity Report (SAR Report) with the federal government when they suspect fraud. Suspicion and not proof is the reporting threshold.

Banks have complete access to the MERS data base where secret endorsements and transfers of authority are routinely hidden and withheld from filing at the Registrar of Deeds Office.

Think about it. If you can find proof of title theft, mortgage fraud, and illegal seizure of your home, why could not those banks and bank approved vendors having far more fraud detection resources at their click and read disposal than you ever did? It is called plausible deniability seated in the forms they fill out, checking the boxes, but absent required due diligence and quality controls. Bank employees are filling out forms, but failing to do the work required of those forms. They thus, imagine they are off the hook for having failed to report the fraud they have enabled, often doing so for a piece of the action or to increase a commission.

CHAPTER SEVEN
The Mortgage Servicer Fraud Partner

Once the fraudsters have control of the property title, they may hire a mortgage servicer company to act as a debt collector. Sometimes attorney offices will function in this role. This transfer of authority is a formal agreement of hire impacting the Deed of Trust as a monetary instrument. Mortgage servicer fraud is a financial crime.

In one case I researched an attorney's office functioned as the aggressive debt collector bullying an elderly couple to abandon their home. The fraud narrative must appear to be superficially true; **under color of law.** Only when one scratches the surface to uncover document fraud does the chain of theft begin to unravel.

In another case a young divorced father died unexpectedly. The inheritance that should have gone to two minor children stole profit from the sale of his home via a phony lien. In this case the lawyer who probated the will and settled the estate had to cooperate. Partnerships between lawyers and REO theft agents, lawyers also acting as REO Investors, are common.

In many schemes house payments no longer go to pay down the principal on the mortgage and may be restyled as assignment of rents. Money no longer flows into the escrow account out of which property taxes and insurance are paid. Income flows into a shell company or a trust entity out of which the fraudsters pay themselves.

Take seriously any intuitive sense you have that something is wrong. Any hire of a new mortgage servicer company or issues claimed to be fixed but continuing to surface are red flags calling for a title theft investigation. Document:

1. Date of conversation(s).
2. Tone of conversation. Reasonable or bullying?
3. Any change in how you are communicated with.
4. Question, who does the caller claim to represent? As title theft moves forward along a specific theft trajectory the mortgage servicer companies may abruptly change hats to function as extortionist debt collectors. They are hired to document the fraud narrative, whatever that is, as true. They will lie claiming to represent the original servicer. Or the lender named in your Deed of Trust.
5. Ask for the full name of the person on the other end of the phone. Trace the name.
6. Ask for and document in your notes the employee number. No employee number is a red flag. Since lies are common phone and verify that the employee number lines up with the name given and the employer that is claimed.
7. Document in your notes the name of any lender, individual, or entity in whose service the attempt to collect unexplained fees, interest payments, back dated forced placed insurance, discrepancies tied to any sudden rise in house payments, etc.
8. The authority of the third-party mortgage servicer company to act as they do rests with

having satisfied themselves that the entity that hired them has possession of a clean, unbroken **chain of title** upon which authority to collect monies must rest. Here is an opportunity not to be squandered to obtain some or all of the title history that no one wants you to see. Demand the title history as proof that any party are validly authorized to act as they do. Understand that there was a contract signed with terms agreed to. Get copies. As the homeowner under a valid Deed of Trust you are lawfully entitled to full disclosure. Ask for proof of whatever authority they claim to act under.

9. A new Note-Owner/Note-Holder has control of the property title. Proof of authority to collect debt should include a copy of;
   (a) The transfer of authority from the secret Note Holder/Note Owner, shell company or proxy identity authorizing the mortgage servicer company to act as they do.
   (b) The hire-contract.
   (c) Declaration that property taxes are current. The paid in full tax receipt from your county becomes a fraud device in the form of an identity theft breeder document. It offers cover in the form of plausible deniability to those hired to perfect some part of the title theft scheme.
   (d) The Title Insurance Policy taken out in the name of the Note-Holder criminal(s) affirms the fictitious ownership, or claims of having a propriety interest in a property

title acquired by robbery. This policy is another fraud device. It is another identity theft breeder document. Offering cover and the excuses; plausible deniability should a federal investigator come calling.
10. Follow up with letters of request escalating to letters of demand that the third-party mortgage servicer company are who they claim to be and have legal authority to act as they do. They must mail you what they said they would send. Failing to do so, even sending useless paper not asked for is a crime. Lack of full disclosure violates the Truth in Lending Act.

Unbelievably I was repeatedly told by multiple entities that I could not have what I asked for. Why? Because complying with my requests for information violated the privacy of the white-collar criminals that hired them. Consider this a flaming red flag and push back. Move up the chain of command. Cite the Truth in Lending Act or whatever else is applicable. Here is a news flash. Those that grease the chain of theft for a RICO Criminal Enterprise are not the victims. It is not they, that need protection.

CHAPTER EIGHT
Document Fraud

Title theft is perfected by **Document Fraud.** Some of these documents appear in the form of signed and notarized **Endorsements**, but will also exist within perjury statement disclaimers, HUD-1 closing documents, the title history put forth by **Title Insurance Companies**, the MERS history of secret filings, and the series of MLS listings.

Appraisal Fraud feature heavily in all Title Theft Schemes. When misleading or inaccurate reports are submitted as part of a loan package, each submission represents a separate crime of mail and, or, wire fraud. This is also bank fraud. Appraisal claims will appear in some of what is filed at the Registrar of Deeds Office. A series of appraisals will increase and decrease valuation as the property title is laundered and the fraud narrative is established.

Identity theft seen in the dual or contradictory claims of ownership are at the click and read disposal of banks. They can easily verify the phony occupancy claims as well as the appraisal history. Unlike the general public, as MERS Members, every lender and the financial services companies have access to the MERS data base and thus to the series of secret transfers, sales, and assigns of authority that are withheld from the Registrar of Deeds Office. Bank employees are part of the fraud crew when they:

1. Fail to question photos that may not match the property details and, or, are clearly downloaded from the internet applying to a different period of time, different MLS Listing, or different address.
2. Fail to vet the appraisal claims of comparable property addresses. Comparable property addresses will appear in the HUD-1 closing documents required of any FHA loan; skimming equity.
3. Fail to investigate arm-in-arm collusion between the buyer and the seller. They may even wrongfully name you as the seller.
4. When they fail to vet the appraisal history against the title insurance history.
5. Fail to recognize when over-valued homes increase fees and commissions of bank employees suggesting cooperation between a corrupt loan officer or underwriter and those that are flipping, laundering the Property Title.
6. Fail to vet for phantom equity, builder buy out schemes and asset rental claims as well as other scams tied to title theft.
7. Fail to see undervalued properties as a red flag to mean that the criminal appraiser may be assisting in a short-sale flip; pure profit to the criminal REO Investor Groups.
8. Undervalued properties perfect home improvement loans with funds not used for the stated purpose.

9. Banks assist title theft when they walk out the appearance of complying with regulations and policies, filling out the required paperwork, but failing to do the work; failing to vet occupancy, valuation, document fraud, chain of property title, former and current title insurance policies, etc.
10. Fail to call you, the resident homeowner alerting to title theft. Fail to do a drive by of the property. Fail to investigate the title theft fraud narrative.

CHAPTER NINE
Closing Agent

Identify the closing agent tied to any loan. Take a hard look at the post illegal seizure sale of your home. Take a hard look at any transfer of ownership via the instrumentality of a Quit Claim Deed or Warranty Deed. Look at all loan closings taking place as flips of the property title, laundering the chain of property title by transferring or selling the home amongst a same buyer to a same seller; Enterprise plus Relationship.

Closing agents are part of the criminal enterprise operations. They are covered by errors and omissions insurance at least up to one million dollars. Add them to your defendant list. Those empowered to act as closing agents include:

1. An attorney or law firm acting as the closing agent.
2. A title company acting as the closing agent.
3. An escrow company acting as the closing agent.

The closing agent name may appear in the body of those documents filed with the Registrar of Deeds Office. Or as a stamp on the upper face of these filings. The closing documents themselves will name them. As always throughout your investigation you are looking to establish Enterprise plus Relationship. Document the partnership between whomever has ordered (hired) the instrumentality of a loan closing and what entity actually conducted the loan closing.

Trace the name and address of that entity that has requested that once assigned an instrument number and filed with the Registrar of Deeds, a copy is mailed back to them. Just as the appraiser performs a needed theft perfecting step so too is the closing agent performing a needed duty, greasing the chain of theft, for criminals. Where fraud is involved add them to your defendant list.

CHAPTER TEN
HUD assigned Number Identifiers

The United States Department of Housing and Urban Development (HUD) assigns REO numbers to approved REO Private Investors. Hiding behind a number identifier in commission of a financial crime is a RICO Predicate Act. After I had read this number in several documents, I was able to connect it to the broker and real estate agent(s) that had targeted my home. REO ID Number 00906148, aka, Vernon Wayne Boyd, aka, the Keller Williams franchise, aka, David Osborn tied to Pretium Partners, LLC. This work led me to the larger group of bad-actors, fleshing out the big picture.

Just to say, I got no help from HUD. They were more interested in concealing mistakes than acting in the public welfare they are obligated to protect.

Based on a forged certificate of abandonment and a signed and notarized perjury disclaimer, my home was fed into a HUD program and then repurchased out of that program by the same REO fraudsters at a greatly reduced price. This occurred three years before the illegal seizure. There was no filing into the public record. No disclosure to me to mean no due diligence. The interim period is when equity is skimmed and house payments are laundered as assignment of rents. This occurred three years before the illegal seizure.

In keeping with lack of legally required disclosure flowing forward to me as the actual resident homeowner HUD failed to file these endorsements at the Registry of Deeds Office. They did not verify the chain of title nor any of the REO-Investor claims over countless other stolen properties. This was the fault of corrupt bureaucrats at the Memphis HUD field office whose actions made the Title Theft – Equity Skimming and trailing Bank Fraud Schemes possible. Investigate beyond the superficial authority claims of any entity you suspect of having failed to do their jobs.

Each time any bank allows equity to be skimmed they are helping to establish the identity theft claims over homes acquired by robbery. There are lots of people and entities from whom potential damages may be sought.

HUD did not file documentation of this sale and transfer where I could find it at the Registrar of Deeds Office. The outcome of this concealment led to Broken Chain of Title. Broken chain of title and document fraud are features of every title theft scam whether complex or simple.

Just as the title insurance claims deceive and mislead, so do these REO number-identifiers offer an excuse to the banks who allow stolen property title to be laundered to say that the work has been done for them. If our government, HUD, says that the fraud narrative is true it must be, right? WRONG! These invitations to laziness are layered into the Bank Theft Delivery System scope of operations described in my book: *Illegal Foreclosure,*

Title Theft, and its Chain of Corruption. Banks willfully avoid the required fraud detection protocols and practices they are mandated by law to follow.

The title theft risk for the financial industry is not a single home. It is title theft of millions – countless numbers of homes feeding the securities industry with new product. You are not a single victim. Do not let anyone dumbing down your case say that you are. Destabilizing private property rights in America is a socialist, communist agenda. Through no fault of your own you were targeted long before you could have ever reasonably recognized that an illegal seizure loomed over the horizon.

The sales pitch that recruits fraud partners to use of the Bank Theft Delivery System is that: *The REO purchasing process can be quicker, far simpler than a regular foreclosure purchase... no lengthy waiting period...* because acquisition of the mortgage as set up for the Property Flip – Equity Skimming Scheme (laundering the chain of title) takes place in secret, no disclosure to homeowners that their property title was just handed over to criminals.

HUD may not have played a role in theft of your home. However, I found proof that as a well-oiled practice HUD programs were easily hijacked by criminals. Only after I'd been evicted from my home did I read, "this is a HUD owned property."

Look for details, little nuggets of information emerging from the paper you read. Do not dismiss something that does not immediately make sense as a mistake. Be flexible and open to the possibility that what you think happened was in fact, far more layered and complex.

CHAPTER ELEVEN
The Fraud Narrative

There is always a **Fraud Narrative**. This is the story that justifies the theft. Think of the fraud narrative as a self-fulfilling prophecy. It appears printed in multiple financial industry sources with no attempt of any party to prove its validity. My research found not even one victim of a mortgage fraud title theft scheme who were phoned or notified by letter to say: Here is the story. Is it true? The fraud narrative is gossip repeated so often that lies overcome the truth. By design, going unchallenged the fraud narrative is just accepted.

Once the fraud narrative is inserted into official records it cannot thereafter be abandoned. It has to be confirmed in the lies that follow. If need be it has to be defended. In other words: *"this is my story and I'm sticking to it come hell or highwater."*

Lies in the form of the fraud narrative is what document fraud is all about.

In my case the fraud narrative stated that I had abandoned my home and lived with my ex-husband in another state. The fraudsters then claimed that a renter was living in my home. Contradicting their own story, the two Keller Williams real estate agents as the secret Note Owners driving my mortgage into default also claimed to be living in my home over that same three-year period.

None of the proof I needed, including the fraud narrative, was immediately evident. I had to dig into the investigation "way leading on to way" as each piece built on another. Just reading this little booklet you are far ahead of where I was when I started.

Violating the Truth in Lending Act as well as the **Bank Secrecy Act**, the system I confronted did their best to avoid telling me the truth. The first people I spoke to, before moving up the chain of authority, did not know the truth. They were just reading off a computer screen. Never get angry with these people. Confide in them and you may find they will act on their own private suspicions and contempt for their employees and help you in unexpected ways.

By willful intent fraud partners:

1. Failed to obtain their own independent title search.
2. Failed to verify occupancy and valuation.
3. Ignored multiple red flags such as types of property title shown. Such as abandoned property claims and type of deed transfers appearing as Warranty Deeds or Quit Claim Deeds.
4. They failed to examine the source documents matched to the phony Note-Holder/Note-Owner claims.
5. Failed to vet for fraud in the Registrar of Deeds Filings matched to the MERS record of secret transfers, sales, and assignments of authority amongst the fraud crew.
6. Failed to compare the title insurance claims to what is filed in the MERS data base.

7. Dates of deed transfers. Multiple deed transfers amongst the same people points to a title theft scheme; laundering the chain of title.
8. Amount and dates of any prior mortgages.
9. Failed to require a signed perjury statement that the documents submitted (including the HUD-1's) are true and accurate.
10. Failed to vet for fraud in same-buyer/same-seller
11. Failed to notify you, the victim of title theft that the digital property title has been hijacked and is being laundered by criminals.

Why would Banks fail consistently to catch, report, and refuse these property flips? The answer is that they put this pipeline of theft in place. They have helped to flip countless numbers of mortgages into the securities market; returning long term profit back to the criminal banks.

All the disclosure you are lawfully entitled to is shut down. Pattern analysis shows that title theft on a grand scale is achieved by conspiracy and cooperation. For title theft to work at multiple junctures where it could be recognized it is not reported.

Whatever the fraud narrative is, it is fitted to your circumstances. Here are some examples.

1. The home was deeded over to the criminal before death.
2. A power of attorney was given over to a lawyer managing the affairs of someone claimed to be vulnerable, true or not, for almost any reason.

3. The property was deeded over in lieu of foreclosure.
4. The homeowner committed to a reverse mortgage and then stopped complying with the agreed upon terms.
5. Be suspicious of documents claimed to be signed by a deceased spouse or parent.
6. The property is abandoned and in derelict condition.
7. Property taxes are not paid.
8. Add on fees are not paid.

Because the property title has to be laundered, flipped amongst the same group of fraudsters, often using family members as straw buyers, there is usually more than one illegal bank loan. Add every party that assisted in moving the chain of theft forward to your defendant list.

1. Every bank
2. Every loan officers
3. Every underwriter
4. Every loan closer
5. Every broker or realtor
6. Every appraiser
7. Every title insurance company.
8. MERSCorp Holdings, Inc., Mortgage Electronic Registration System generally known as MERS.
9. Any foreclosure mill attorney or substitute trustee perfecting title theft for their clients.

CHAPTER TWELVE
Laundering the Digital Property Title

When the REO Investors step in to pay property taxes on a mortgage they have just acquired by fraud, this establishes a layer of identity theft authority over the mortgage. The criminal "investor" becomes the Note-Holder of record. Homeowners have no idea that a change has taken place.

You cannot verify fictitious claims and authority which you are not privy to. This is the fault of those that fail to report, disclose, investigate or verify proof of title.

For these schemes to operate as they do, victims of title theft must be disenfranchised from any ability to fight back. Think about it. If you had any of the information you were legally entitled to, you would report the assault upon your property title and upon you personally.

Once the fraudster(s) has control over the **digital property title** they can layer the identity theft claims into multiple records. When this has been accomplished to the extent that others will recklessly accept the lies and fictitious history a, major goal in the theft trajectory is achieved.

**Control over the digital property title
PRE-DATES illegal seizure or any
foreclosure charade and is accomplished by
Document Fraud.**

Your job is NOT to be the sitting duck that title theft criminals expect you to be. During the interim period that the digital property title is being electronically laundered it is hoped that by omission of what is secreted away in the MERS E-Registry System and data base you are disenfranchised from fighting back.

This interim period between acquisition and control over the digital property title, up to the illegal seizure, is very lucrative for the criminal enterprise. This is the period that the property title is laundered and equity is skimmed. Transfers of the property title amongst the same bad actors may include a simple Deed Transfer. It may include a short sale, a home improvement loan, theft of HUD resources, and almost always illegal bank loans. This is also the period where house payments and tacked on illegal servicing fees are laundered in year-end filings as rental income. At some point in the chain of theft you are transformed from a homeowner under a valid Deed of Trust to a renter. None of the requisite title transfers take place in a vacuum. None of this proof is filed where you can find it. You are entirely disenfranchised from all legally required disclosures. This interim period is replicated multiple times over per theft of countless other homes.

You are looking to establish **Broken Chain of Title.** Start with demanding the full MERS History. Read chapter nineteen and Part 111 of my book: *Illegal Foreclosure, Title Theft, and its Chain of Corruption*.

You will see that some of the same fraud partners fill multiple roles. This reduces the risk of exposure but may also make your job easier. In my case the Note-Holder were two Keller Williams Realtors who claimed to be living in my home during the three-year period that the Property Title was laundered.

Get to the place where you can name each person within the local group. They function as the perpetrator nexus.

For a fee, commission, or piece of the action everyone works in tandem to accomplish the goals of the criminal enterprise. Become conversant in describing the specific chain of theft as it impacted you personally. Report these crimes to local law enforcement and also to state and federal regulatory offices. To the FBI local field office and where lawyers are involved to the bar association. There are multiple junctures where title theft could be stopped in its tracks. Hold lenders, mortgage servicer companies, trustees, closing agents, and others accountable, naming them as defendants in any lawsuit you file. They failed to:

1. Take in hand the trail of endorsements filed at the Registrar of Deeds Office vetting for forgery.
2. Failed to compare endorsement claims with the title insurance claims and what is concealed from the public within the MERS E-Registry System.
3. Failed to vet for forgery, lies, and discrepancies with what is known about how title theft operates.
4. Failed to follow the chain of title.

5. For having blindly accepted the title insurance lies performing no independent review.
6. Failed to see flips of the property title amongst the same parties as a red flag pointing to a property flip scheme; laundering the chain of title for the same reason that drug assets and other illegally acquired assets are laundered.
7. Failed to verify that the seller holds the title.
8. Failed to verify that any buyer is not a straw buyer acting to flip the property title back to the criminal entity under the pretense of a legitimate transaction.
9. Failed to apply needed scrutiny to those using the moniker "REO Investors" or "Private Investors" or "Institutional Investors" as flaming red flags.
10. When banks recognize fraud using HUD REO Numbers as an identifier, and fail to report this fraud back to HUD they are enabling the unlawful hijacking of federal programs meant to benefit the poor and paid for with tax dollars.

When any party works in concert to conceal the perpetrator identities to thus, deprive victims of recognition of how and by whom they are being scammed. When they fail to report bank fraud, document fraud, and other crimes, they become part of the Criminal Enterprise Operations.

Enterprise plus relationship makes each equally liable.
Add them to your defendant list.

11. Failed to confirm occupancy claims.
12. Failed to investigate the fraud narrative as the premise for how the home was lost, flipped and repurchased by the same parties.
13. Failed to document and vet the source of funds arriving into county and state coffers; including funds that pay property taxes.

During the interim period that the property title is being laundered, it is NOT that the property taxes are NOT paid. It is that they are NO LONGER paid under the terms of your Deed of Trust from an escrow account.
Think about it.
This is a distinction with a huge difference!
If your county notified you that the taxes were not paid under the terms of a former Deed of Trust you would want to know why.
Thus, in more complex schemes the fraudsters are very careful to pay these taxes. They do so in the secret Note-Holder/Note-Owner name or in the name of a shell company or proxy. The paid in full county tax receipt becomes an identity theft breeder document as a direct result of states failure to keep up with the growth of these crimes, protecting the public welfare.

14. Failed to vet the appraisal history.
15. Failed to understand the role each party is hired to perform matched against any theft agenda of those that hire them.
16. Banks that fail to file Suspicious Activity Reports (SAR). Suspicion of fraud and not proof being the threshold for filing these reports.
17. Failed to notify you, the resident homeowner, that identity theft operating as a possible title theft scheme is in the works. Add them to your defendant list.

CHAPTER THIRTEEN
Lack of Disclosure is Strategic and Deliberate

The arrogant assumption, seated in the complete lack of legally required disclosure flowing in your direction confirms that no one is watching. Thus, we can assert that title theft is an inside job. The fraudsters believe that you and all other targets of title theft will never learn enough that you can fight back.

The question you must answer becomes. How does each example of document fraud, each failure to vet for fraud, and the role played by each party invalidate everything that comes before and after?

Obtaining an assignment through fraudulent means invalidates the assignment. Fraud destroys the validity of everything into which it enters. It vitiates the most solemn contracts, documents, and even judgments. Walker v. Rich, 70 Cal. App. 139 (Cal.App.1926).

By law REO Investors are to sell these homes on the open market. The rigged system enabled by MERS and networked to select realtors and brokers has meant that average citizens are cut out as back door deals, illegal appraisals, and price fixing rule the day. Go back and look at what is filed at the Registrar of Deeds Office. Only after it is considered safe will the criminal identity surface in the public record.

CHAPTER FOURTEEN
Title Theft is an Identity Theft Crime

In title theft **Identity Theft** is accomplished with three key **Breeder Documents**. Each moves the chain of theft forward at a specific juncture. Each is used to establish criminal claims of ownership replacing your authority with that of the criminal identity.

As a pattern of practice other names appearing in endorsements hide the actual criminal Note-Holder/Note-Owner identity. If you cannot name those that have targeted the home for theft, you cannot effectively fight back. These misrepresentations of identity, where they appear, render these endorsements fraud devices.

Believe nothing you read until proven true. No one expects you to push back and ask questions. Names that commonly conceal the criminal identity may appear as that of the:

1. The Original Lender
2. The Original Servicer
3. A defunct company
4. The foreclosure arm of a bank
5. Shell companies
6. Trust vehicles
7. Straw buyers and almost always...
8. Mortgage Electronic Registration System, MERS-Corp Holdings, Inc. or any version of the MERS name.

9. Your name may appear as signing something like a power of attorney that in fact you never signed.

As an example, I only ever read Bank of America as the foreclosing party. In fact, there was no foreclosure since Bank of America had off-loaded my mortgage to criminals three years before. Bank of America then entered into a conspiracy to conceal this event thereby, protecting the theft partnerships.

Three breeder documents establish the criminal claims of ownership and authority over homes acquired by robbery. We will look at each separately.

These three breeder documents are the buildup that will enable the illegal seizure in whatever form that takes. In the order that they usually appear they are:

1. The county Property Tax Receipt noted as having been paid in full by the criminal identity or a proxy tied to that identity, usually takes place at the start of the Property Flip, Equity Skimming, Title Theft Scheme.
2. The Title Insurance Policy taken out in the name of the fraudster.
3. The Assignment of the Deed of Trust.

County Property Tax Receipt: Proof that taxes are paid becomes part of any loan package needed to launder your property title. Every transaction that goes off without a challenge creates more distance between your claims and those of the criminals. The source of funds that pay these taxes come from the REO Investor criminal enterprise and can be traced by you. When a change like this takes place, sadly (dangerously) all that your county trustee is trained to care about is that taxes are paid.

Taxes paid in full is a juncture in the theft trajectory that you and others could be notified that a change has taken place and if need be take steps to defend your property rights. County job descriptions and fraud detection training has not kept up with the massive growth of title theft. If this keeps up counties will be subject to law suits in proportion to the numbers of victims that wake up and fight back and the numbers of lawyers that decide to specialize in this field.

Among the pieces of information, you need is that approximate date that the complicit bank allowed the fraudsters to assume your mortgage; no disclosure to you. That event can be informed by the date that the county in which you live allowed a RICO Criminal Enterprise to pay your property taxes with dirty money. Doing so with no effective fraud detection practices in place. No warning that your property title is under possible attack. Ask yourself, who does it serve not to close these theft perfecting loopholes?

County property tax receipts in the name of the fraudsters or whatever shell company or proxy-identity they hide behind are used to undermine and interfere with the Deed of Trust. The Deed of Trust and Promissory Note is a valid contract between you and the lender. Everything that comes after is a theft perfecting fraud device greasing the chain of theft. The act of destroying rights under contract for financial gain is called **Tortious Interference**.

Proof that taxes are paid in full is one piece that allow the criminal(s) to hire the third-party mortgage servicer company, foreclosure mill attorney, a lawyer that will act as the new **Substitute Trustee**, as well as other fraud perfecting services. Why? Because the county in which you live has just handed the criminals an identity theft fraud device. When this dirty money changes hands and the criminal claims are rubber stamped, the chain of theft can move toward the goal of illegal seizure. Each time this receipt is mailed or wired to another entity this is an example of mail or wire fraud. Each separate instance is an unlawful RICO predicate act.

In my case there was also a mail clearing center in the picture pretending to be Bank of America and using Bank of America letterhead; controlling the flow of communication. **Mail and wire fraud** feature heavily in all title theft schemes. List and document every example.

The comptroller of the currency in your state and the county trustee elected or appointed to collect property taxes should be fully on board with helping you. You want copies of every cancelled check or any funds transfer directly wired into any state or county bank account falling within and helping to establish the theft time line of events. Why? Because under law the source of dirty money in this country matters enormously.

Title Insurance Company. There is no sale, no skimming equity via bank fraud absent a Title Insurance Policy. The title insurance claims sell lenders on the idea that the work has been done for them. They assert to loan officers, any loan closers, and underwriters that this is a property title free of fraud, doubt, errors, and forgery.

A selling point to banks, mortgage companies, and other fraud enablers is that the Title Insurance Company will take the hit if title theft or some other financial fraud is proven. In mafia terms they act as the bag-men. They are the layer of distance that facilitates the flow of money coming from "same" seller to "same" buyer. Coming from the financial institution back to the criminal entity as interim loans are secured and money is skimmed.

Like the property tax receipts title insurance will prop up and, in all effect, certify broken chain of title as somehow being acceptable. Putting forward to banks the lie that the criminal Note-Holder/Note-Owner has passed the smell test when nothing could be further from the truth. These companies are insured under their own errors and omissions policies. They are bank approved vendors. Enterprise plus Relationship. Add them to your defendant list.

The title insurance policy, like the HUD-1, will vomit up a wealth of information. This information will allow you to flesh out the fraudster identities. It will tie the local footprint of operations to the national footprint.

The Assignment of the Deed of Trust: This breeder document will be openly filed at the Registrar of Deeds Office. Although the language is deceptive, it assigns the preexisting rights to your home from you to the criminal entity. As a fraud tool it is filed without actually naming the criminal Note-Owner identity. Pick up the phone and call whomever it was that filed this Assignment asking for the Note-Owner identity. You likely will be lied to, but document the ask in your notes and ask away. Again, and again...

The physical seizure of what has long been a digital theft asset cannot take place without this filing. According to McDonnell Property Analytics. *"...it has been standard industry practice for mortgage servicers filing foreclosure actions to submit false affidavits, fraudulently backdated documents and other fraudulent documents in court for, at least the past fifteen years. In addition to false affidavits, mortgage servicers have also fabricated mortgage assignments and other documents on behalf of entities that no longer exist."*[1]

Where title theft is the game the Assignment of the Deed of Trust is a theft perfecting conveyance document. Appearance in the public record is required by law. As one of the three key identity theft breeder documents, like the others it greases the chain of theft and is thus, a complete nullity. Every endorsement that trails after this endorsement is void; having no power to enforce. Every entity that relied upon its use, but failed to examine a complete chain of title failed to apply basic due diligence requirements. They ignored the Property Flip Equity Skimming red flags that banks are extensively trained to recognize and report.

Following the Assignment of the Deed of Trust a corrupt substitute trustee will produce the fraud device of a Substitute Trustee's Deed.

---

[1] From: City of Seattle Review of Mortgage Documents © 2015 McDonnell Analytics, Inc., Appendix "1" Definition of Terms. Marie McDonnell is an acknowledged expert in the field of mortgage fraud and title theft.

Payment of property taxes by criminals precedes the filing of the Assignment of the Deed of Trust. Take this document in hand and make an immediate beeline to the county tax office. Who has been paying the property taxes? The first answer will be woefully and superficially wrong. You are not asking for an opinion, but for documentation. States are so remiss in protecting against dirty money that you will have to push for the paper and payment history.

Take what you find from the property tax payment(s) history and next ask for a copy of every title insurance policy tied to any flip or loan. These three Breeder Documents will help you flesh out the chain of theft. The start, the interim period, the illegal seizure and after.

CHAPTER FIFTEEN
Fraud Partner – Substitute Trustee

Depending on how many prior flips of the property title have taken place, there will be a replacement **Substitute Trustee**. There may even be a third Resubstituted Trustee.

Appointment of a Substitute Trustee filing will name both the former trustee named in your Deed of Trust and the replacement trustee acting as part of the fraud crew. The replacement trustee is presiding over and facilitating some of the final steps in the chain of theft. The series of endorsements created by and tied to the fraudster-trustee, appear in this order.

1. **Assignment of the Deed of Trust** (Identity theft breeder document). Does a batch number appear? To mean that multiple homes are being set up for illegal seizure at the same time pointing to a more sophisticated chain of theft; filed by the same foreclosure mill attorneys. Get the batch list of other property addresses. Research into other homes will make up a very powerful pattern example grouping. To prove that you are not the sole victim. Link each property to the same perpetrator nexus.
2. **Appointment of Substitute Trustee** (replacing a former trustee). This endorsement replaces the first trustee named in your Deed of Trust. This is a legal transfer of authority granted by the secret Note-Holder/Note-Owner to a

partner in crime. When legal documents are used to perfect a crime the documents themselves are fraud devices. They have no power to enforce.

3. **Substitute Trustee's Deed.** This new Deed allows for a Trustee Sale. Now the fraudster-trustee is authorized to sell the physical premises of a home for the criminal clients. The criminal clients have had previous control over the digital property title and now, having driven the mortgage into default, they can perfect an illegal seizure via the trustee sale. A major goal in the theft trajectory is now accomplished.

Pick up the phone and call any substitute trustee. Ask if there have been other interim trustees named in filings concealed in the MERS System. How often have they been hired to function as trustee by the REO Investors or the Foreclosure Mill, Attorneys? What other properties? If there is nothing to hide, nothing will be hidden. Start out with polite inquiry moving on to:

1. Demand a copy of the hire contract they signed. If names or content is redacted demand full disclosure.
2. Who actually hired the Trustee? The first answer will likely default back to your original lender or to a company like Core Logic.
3. Who do they consider to be the client?
4. How is the trustee being paid for services rendered?
5. Demand a copy of what masquerades as a complete property title history given over to the Substitute Trustee as authority for the hire.

Get in the habit of asking the same question more than once, just rephrased differently. Push back against the automatic "NO."

The authority of any Trustee rests on a clean, unbroken, and complete chain of title free of fraud, error, doubt, and forgery. The trustee has a duty to act as an honest administrator. I found that some even acted in a dual capacity as the foreclosure mill attorneys keeping the circle of risk tight and lean, but also making your job easier. Where arm-in-arm criminal collusion, when even the mere appearance of such exists, it is your right to request (demand) a new trustee.

Lawyers are averse to perjuring themselves in any context that produces a record. If you find yourself in court demand that the trustee appear. When a trustee is shielded from showing up, this a red flag. Ask the judge to replace the current trustee with an honest administrator having no conflicts of interest.

1. They may be tied to the same law firm that owns the title company as an arm of the title theft operations.
2. They may be the actual and same closing agent making no attempt to vet the identity theft claims and acting as part of the fraud crew.
3. They may have presided over previous sales, assigns, and transfers of authority laundering the chain of title while, for a piece of the action, skimming equity.
4. They may not even be an actual person. Some endorsements are created out of whole cloth.

CHAPTER SIXTEEN
Instruments of Attack

In any murder investigation paramount on the mind of any homicide detective is the murder weapon. Both finger prints and DNA may be lifted from the weapon of choice tracing back to that person that wielded the fatal blow. Or, if a murder for hire and upon investigation will reveal that criminal that paid for the hit job.

It is the same with title theft. As the detective proving a series of crimes, you need to find the murder weapon. The weapons are the (document fraud) instrumentality used to perfect the theft. Always be mindful that some of the endorsements you are legally entitled to are by design and intent, secreted away in the theft facilitating MERS System. Documents may also be held back from filing by a complicit title company, loan closer, or ambiguously titled, so called asset manager. Ask the Registrar of Deeds in your county for help. They should write letters that are copied to you asking for any withheld filings that may have compromised their recordation system leading to Broken Chain of Title. No help from any elected bureaucrat or any of the staff is a red flag; something to hide.

Endorsements used as fraud devices, greasing the chain of theft, may include any combination of the following signed and notarized instruments selectively weaponized, fitted to the fraud narrative, perfecting theft of your home.

1. Deed in Lieu of Foreclosure
2. Quit Claim Deed
3. Warranty Deed
4. Power of Attorney
5. Assignment of the Deed of Trust
6. Assignment of any Substitute Trustee or Resubstituted Trustee
7. Deed of Trust
8. Notice of Lis Pendens
9. Any lien claiming a, financial interest in the property

Gathering Documentation

1. Begin by copying all documents on file with the Registrar of Deeds Office in your county. Start with the **Source Documents.**
2. Every instrument that appears under your name and address.
3. If two or more persons signed the Deed of Trust at the time of purchase, search under every signer name. In doing this I found that something like a forged Power of Attorney was filed under the second name listed, or a version of that name, but not under the first name listed in the Deed of Trust. Expect that these people are very devious and practiced at covering their tracks.
4. Search under common misspellings of your name. Reversal of names. Elevated middle

names. Anything to corrupt or impede the data search and thus, to conceal document fraud. Not, Nancy Linsey Smith, but N. Lindsey Smith, or Smith Lindsey. Doing this work is time consuming. Plan for a lunch break, take your time, and settle in at the computer terminal at the Registrar of Deeds Office.

5. If doing this work from home copy to a file on your computer.
6. Copy all documents filed with the Assessor Office. The start of the appraisal history begins with claim of value upon which taxes are levied.
7. Copy the complete MLS Listing history, both public and non-public.
8. Download any photos of your home appearing over the internet on sites like Zillow as well as the descriptions and appraisal claims.

NEXT Examine these documents. You are looking for any claim that reads other than it should or proposes an event that you were not physically present for. Or, were never notified of during that time that you lived in your home or immediately after. The accumulated details that might otherwise be dismissed as a simple error proves intent to deceive.

1. Have the endorsements been signed?
2. Have they been notarized?
3. Does the signer name read differently from any claim in the body of the document?
4. Check all dates against the theft time line you develop.

5. Look for alternative dates / back dated or forward dated.
6. Outright lies
7. Absent or corrupted, smudged signatures
8. Is there a clearly typed name and title appearing beneath any hard to read signature as a tool to conceal the signature identity?
9. Any signature that is no more than a scrawl but is allowed as a valid identifier in some states. See this as a red flag.
10. Any smudged and messy looking document is a red flag to mean that this may be a repurposed fraud device used to steal homes other than your own.

For about three years I paid a monthly fee to use an online investigative service, worth every penny. If information dries up the criminals may have scrubbed their information from the site you are using. When you suspect this has happened research other options and switch over to a new identity theft back ground service.

You may find that some names are ghosts. They might as well be the teenage bag boy at the grocery store. You will likely find **Robosigners.** You may read a name, make a phone call only to find that this person denies they signed the endorsements. Or denies that they played any role in creating the security instruments. Look into the:

1. Background of every signer
2. Every company and individual name appearing in these documents

3. Identify the closing agent
4. Any lawyer playing multiple roles
5. Any bank or lender
6. Any mortgage servicer company named
7. Defunct companies, persons, and entities no longer in business
8. Any party claiming to be an "asset manager."
9. Notaries that upon investigation claim to have never witnessed and affixed their seal to endorsements on file.

Where fraud is involved many of these signers claiming to have authority cannot be produced as walking breathing people. Others cannot show up in any court of law unless they are willing to perjure themselves.

UPON INVESTIGATION some are **Robosigners**. Stacks of endorsements are placed before the signer. Working with a complicit notary in assembly line fashion the phony endorsements are blindly signed and notarized. Some robosigners appear as MERS Signing Officers claiming to be vice-presidents of MERSCorp Holding, Inc., when in fact they are vice-president of nothing. The same is true of the HUD-1.

Some signers are found to be working directly as employees or family members of the white-collar criminals. Again... when challenged to give testimony these signers cannot show up in court without committing perjury and risking jail time. Something appearing as legal is not legal if the end goal is theft of private property operating **Under Cover of Law**.

CHAPTER SEVENTEEN
Confusion

The practice of sowing confusion, under the guise of innocent mistakes is a very common fraud tool used to deflect the truth. Where you find one such error there will be others. These errors expose the pattern of practice matched to how you were profiled.

In one example a Power of Attorney was claimed to have been signed by an elderly parent at a point in time when she was comatose and dying in a hospital. Other siblings living out of state were just expected to accept this. In another, a debt covered under a former bankruptcy proceeding was resurrected providing the secret Note-Holder with a ready fraud narrative as to why he had rights under the guise of a fabricated and fictitious lien.

A picture of how title theft practices work, sowing lies and confusion into endorsements comes from a case filed by two Tennessee lawyers; Eugene N. Bulso, Jr. and Paul J. Krog. *REO Family Trust Services, LLC and Billy Gregory vs REO Holdings, LLC; Charles E. Walker; Jon Paul Johnson; Julie Coone, and Merdan Ibrahim, Defendants.* Chapter twenty-five of the book, *Illegal foreclosure, Title theft, and its Chain of corruption* quotes from one of their case filings. In this case we have a picture of how subtle and overt misstatements are layered into the record to thus render those endorsements fraud tools, null and void, with no power to enforce.

"The Gomez Quitclaim and Gomez Affidavits are forgeries. Clarissa Gomez, if such a person exist, is not Clarice Gomez, the daughter of Manuel Martin, and did not sign the Gomez Quitclaim or the Gomez Affidavit in any event."

And: *"The Booker Affidavit is false and fraudulent several times over. First, the son of Betty Burns was not named Allen Booker, but was instead named Allen Booher: The Booker Affidavit is thus false as to its principal contention, that the affiant is the son of Betty Burns. Second, no one by either name, Allen Booker or Allen Booher, resides at 102 Park Avenue, Piscataway, New Jersey, 08854: indeed, no one resides at this address, which is a vacant lot."*

Continues: *Third, even Allen Booker did not sign the Booker Affidavit: his signature was electronically or photostatically copied from a 1992 deed of record with Middlesex County, New Jersey, County Clerk at Book 3974, Page 824."*

Whether a family member trying to figure out how and why they did not inherit, whether a lawyer seeking the truth, or an investigator with a badge most are slow to this fight. Reading this little booklet, you recognize the big picture. Whittle away to see what fits. That your home was stolen, regardless of how the chain of theft transpired, is a crime impacting millions of Americans.

CHAPTER EIGHTEEN
Notary Fraud

I was shocked to find so many examples of notary fraud. Tie any notary you suspect of fraud to the criminal enterprise group of bad actors. Apply your newly developed skills of skepticism and scrutiny. Confirm:

1. Does the Notary claim to have signed and applied the notary seal?
2. Who did the Notary work for at the time the document was claimed to be notarized?
3. As a red flag is there a gap between when an instrument was signed by the parties and when it was claimed to be notarized?
4. At the time, was the Notary current on their license?
5. Is the notary stamp smudged? Is it clean and readable?
6. As a very common practice, has the notary seal and notaries signature been lifted from another document and *photostatically* affixed to another.
7. Call the notary. Does the entry appear as proper in the notary book? If not, you are looking at forgery.
8. Do the last digits in the year appear smudged and, or, replaced?

9. Was every party physically present at the time of signing?
10. By what means did the Notary confirm identity? Were these identity claims properly entered into the notary book?
11. Dates are both forward dated and back dated. Wrong and fictitious dates render any endorsement a fraud device.
12. Regard as a red flag any signed statement, "I hereby certify as true" appearing on the face of any document pretending to substitute for an actual notary stamp and signature. See the Power of Attorney example pictured in Part 111 of my book: *Illegal Foreclosure, Title Theft, and its Chain of Corruption.*

CHAPTER NINETEEN
Create a Visual

Take each document in hand and create for yourself a visual. Work parallel across the page. In the first cell identify the type of endorsement. Warranty Deed, Deed in Lieu of Foreclosure, Quit Claim Deed, etc. In the next cell write the instrument number. Go across the page as seen in the example below. Add other cells as may be indicated. Affix your summary to the facing page of every document adding your notes below.

You are looking for Enterprise plus Relationship. There is the local fraud crew and then there is the national footprint of operatives. Add as indicated to your perp wall.

TYPE OF FILING	INST. No.	WHERE signed?	DATE signed	
Warranty Deed	000	Texas	6/1/2021	
GRANTOR	**GRANTEE**	NOTARY Name and State	Notary Date	Once filed "Return to"
N. Smith	Zero, LLC	J. Dupe Florida	8/25/21	Blank Title Co.

Here are some red flags gleaned from this simple exercise, but also found in other examples related to different instruments.

1. This Warranty Deed was signed in Texas but your home as the property address is located in Florida.
2. The title company is found by you to be owned (connected) to a foreclosure mill attorney.
3. The notary license resides in Florida, not Texas where the endorsement is claimed to be signed.
4. It is unlikely that the **Grantor** and the **Grantee** were present in the same room. Ask, how did the notary verify the identity of each signer present? As a red flag why wasn't a local notary used? Law offices, title and escrow companies, all banks have notaries on staff. Use of an out of state notary creates a level of distance only needed by those committing document fraud and possibly pointing to a notary signature and seal lifted from another filing.
5. J. Dupe, as the Notary can verify none of the information certified by the notary seal and signature. Is this a robosigned endorsement; having no power to enforce?
6. This Warranty Deed was signed two months before it was notarized begging the question: Is this a notary signature and seal lifted from another document and photostatically affixed to the fraud device of this Warranty Deed?
7. The Grantor is not you. At the time that this transfer of your property took place you were still living in your home totally disenfranchised and cut off from all legally required disclosure.

8. Zero, LLC as the Grantee receiving the property is found to be a shell company. What are they hiding and who does this brick wall protect? Where is this company registered? Are they licensed to do business within your state? <u>Go to the Secretary of State web page and conduct a search; printing off the company details.</u> What parent company registered the shell company, very likely traced to Delaware?

9. The Warranty Deed will be used to commit bank fraud. After any Warranty Deed or Quit Claim Deed appears, the fraudsters may apply for a last bank loan. Or the home may be sold outright and, or, transferred into the shell company as set up for securities fraud. Some REO Investors build their rental portfolio by keeping some of these homes diverting from the Bank Theft Delivery System they were illegally expected to follow as the very specific and easily recognized chain of theft. Many of these rental homes end up managed by the same REO Investor Groups.

Remember. Transfer of your mortgage or ownership rights to criminals with no disclosure to you takes place before any of the fraud perfecting endorsements are filed into the public record. Some are concealed in the MERS System. Others are withheld by complicit local title companies or closing agents. Thus, everything filed that has established the identity theft claims, corrupted the source document(s), and pushed forward the chain of theft is a fraud device; having no power to enforce.

CHAPTER TWENTY
The Perp Wall

A crime has been committed. Create a perp wall. A perp wall is a visual that fleshes out Enterprise plus Relationship. It will help establish the theft time line; beginning, interim period, and end. The end is reached only when the goals of the criminal enterprise are met.

Begin by writing out a label for those services that played some role in perfecting the theft of your home. As your investigation proceeds match that label to the bad actor co-conspirators. This is what my perp wall came to look like. Take what fits from this list and leave the rest.

1. The mail clearing center; Stewart Lender Services. Write a label for: MAIL CLEARING CENTER.
2. The insurer grantor claiming no fraud in the title history. For me it was First American Title Insurance Company. Write a label for: TITLE INSURANCE COMPANY.
3. The Mortgage Servicer Company hired by the secret Note-Holder/Note Owner. May be an extortionist debt collector. A primary duty is to drive the mortgage into default while bullying you to walk away. They don't work for you, nor do they work for your original lender. Create a label for: MORTGAGE SERVICER COMPANY(s).
4. A money manager is needed. In my case it was a Certified Public Accountant living five homes

away from me. These crimes have both a local and national footprint of operation. Create a label that reads: MONEY MANAGER.
5. A HUD licensed appraiser who is also licensed by your state to thus limit exposure keeping the circle tight and lean. In my case there were two known appraisers. One was a Keller Williams broker; issuing, Broker Price Opinions. This man was also the secret Keller Williams broker and Note-Holder also masquerading as Bank of America. Create a label for APPRAISER(s).
6. Write out labels for REALTOR(s), BROKER(s), Real Estate Company(s).

Once you have been evicted or otherwise threatened to leave the home (or utterly ambushed) two real estate companies will conspire; flipping the home back to the REO secret Note-Owner/Note-Holder.

To conceal that the buyer is also the seller they may hide behind that of a straw buyer.

The first MLS listing is not made public. It conceals the name of the person or entity that has had secret possession of the digital property title but now, having successfully laundered the property title will perfect the illegal seizure of your home.

In this very common scenario, or some adaptation thereof, the first MLS listing will transfer the listing of the home to the decoy realty company. The decoy realty company will be the public face of the listing. They will facilitate one of the last, but crucial flips of the property title back to the secret client whose listing they represent. As always, the Note Owner name has to be concealed from you. The decoy realty companies help out. They should be named in any lawsuit you file.

This partnership between the two realty companies contrive that no random member of the public can purchase what has been a theft asset for a very long time. Two realty companies hide the arm-in-arm criminal collusion that price fixes any apparent sale while flipping the theft asset (your home) back to the same criminal enterprise. Look for and document these connections.

7. Your investigation will lead you to those that have been creating the fraud perfecting signed and notarized endorsements. This could be an individual, title company, or attorney(s). It could be almost anyone sitting at a computer and ordering up the required forms. Write out and pin to your perp wall, DOCUMENT FRAUD AUTHOR(s).

8. The Substitute Trustee whom you will link to the secret Note-Holder / Note-Owner that hired them and, or, to the mafia like activities of the Foreclosure Mill attorneys. This is not the trustee named in your original Deed of Trust. That trustee has to be replaced with a co-operating fraud partner. Write a label for the SUBSTITUTE TRUSTEE.

9. Ownership was transferred to the criminal via the actions of a closing agent. Create labels for TITLE COMPANY and CLOSING AGENT. There may be more than one. The first flip may have been perfected by the ESCROW Company directed by the lender and transferring control

over your mortgage to the REO Investors at the start of the title theft scheme. The next by a title company local to the core group of perpetrators. Add to your perp wall over time as indicated by what your investigation produces.

10. Straw buyer. Did the property end up as a rental? Write a label for: STRAW BUYER. In year-end tax filings the straw buyer will usually be styled as a renter.
11. The ultimate destination. Did the white-collar criminals keep the home, or sell it and pocket the cash? Or was the home transferred to a company like the Blackstone Group or Pretium Partners, LLC operating under shell companies in different states. Or did it go to a large corporate owner of rental property? Write a label for: ULTIMATE DESTINATION.

Again... for a more complete picture of title theft schemes, how they work and other avenues of investigation, read my book: ***Illegal Foreclosure, Title Theft, and its Chain of Corruption.***

Under the guise of urban or rural "development" any sudden rise in property taxes over a targeted neighborhood is a red flag. Various adaptations of title theft use property taxes as the prelude and set up for illegal seizures over selected blocks of territory. These practices drive at risk populations out of a neighborhood slated for "improvement" and into homelessness. These schemes require the cooperation of corrupt bureaucrats working with corporate investors. A **bribe** in one form or another is involved.

CHAPTER TWENTY-ONE
Prove What You Say

Follow up every request with a letter clearly stating what it is that you have asked for. Letters are the official means of communication. If you find yourself in court letters, journal entries, and phone call logs carry a lot of weight. Always be mindful of cementing your position via real-time documentation. I could usually prove whom I talked with, when the conversation took place and what was promised. I could then document outcome or complete lack of outcome since more often than not I was at first ignored, lied to, and underestimated.

No one expects you to be organized. Staying organized means that you can lay your hands on what you need when you need it. If money is tight re-purpose some of what you may already have sitting around or ask friends for help in acquiring the basic list of office supplies.

Here is a get started list of supplies:

- One plastic file box.
- It may not seem you need them, but buy a box of standard weight three ring sheet protectors.
- Large paper clips are preferred.
- Hanging folders.
- File folders.

- Sticky labels for folders.
- Start with one three ring, two inch "Heavy Duty" binder.
- Three ring content dividers; table of content dividers with tabs.
- For your perp wall a cork bulletin board or something serving the same purpose, and push pins.

CHAPTER TWENTY-TWO
Okay to be a Nag

My last bit of advice about the proof you accumulate is this: NEVER GIVE ANY ATTORNEY THE ORIGINAL COPIES of anything.

Even if you start out trusting them not to be bought off by the other side. Induced to mitigate (limit) your case for a piece of the action or a quick pay day; please, please, please do protect and guard your own, independently kept set of records. If you've read my book you know that I trusted the wrong persons. Know the ethical requirements that dictate the lawyer-client relationship.

Any lawyer that tells you not to file a police report cannot be trusted. Just as you would report a stolen car, your ownership rights per title theft are in the same category. It is easier to steal a home than it is to steal a car in this country. Say so, get the theft on record and file that police report. The fraudsters you identify have hijacked federal programs, interfered with ongoing investigations, and as instigators of these crimes are the banks and financial institutions that we have trusted.

CHAPTER TWENTY-THREE
There are Laws

Your mortgage was off loaded to criminals, no disclosure to you, who then reconfigured the terms of that debt for the sole purpose of driving your mortgage into default. Your Deed of Trust and, or, Promissory Note documented the terms of the debt secured by the physical premises of the home. The <u>Truth in Lending Act</u> was passed in 1968 protecting consumers from deceptive language regarding debt and cost of credit.

My first red flag was an abrupt rise in my house payment by $300.00. This was the act of the secret Note-Holder who now had power to drive my mortgage into default. My next red flag was forced placed insurance. Not until it was too late would I realize I was not dealing with Bank of America. I was communicating with the Mortgage Servicer hired by the secret REO Note-Holders masquerading as Bank of America.

Any entity that acquires a mortgage or pool of mortgages also acquire the debt. They are legally liable to follow state and federal laws. Many states have added penalties for white collar crimes committed against the elderly. When the fraudster entity assumes your mortgage for the sole purpose of committing title theft this is very obviously a crime.

Though you may not have recognized it as such, there is almost always an illegal search of your home preceding the illegal seizure. Illegal search and seizure are violations of the <u>Fourth Amendment to the U.S. Constitution</u>. Gaining access for appraisal purposes under false pretenses is an illegal search in preparation for the upcoming illegal seizure.

Be extremely wary of any person coming up with any excuse to view the interior of your home. Ask for business cards. Walk outside and using your cell phone take a photo of the license plate. Document the make and model of the vehicle and of course whoever it was that knocked on the door and asked for access. Take their picture as well.

Theft of a home is no different from the chop-shop sale of auto parts, gold melted down from stolen jewelry, the resale of stolen guns and electronics via the conduit of a pawn shop. These are all crimes punishable under law; sending people to jail. These laws say that no one can give (sell) what they do not own. No person or entity receiving or buying stolen goods can claim rightful ownership over that property. **"The baseline principal of our system of property regarding transfers of ownership is nemo data quad non habit – "no one can give what he does not have."** City of Seattle Review of Mortgage Documents, Definition of Terms, McDonnell Analytics, Inc.

This brings us to the Racketeer Influenced Corrupt Organizations Act (RICO). Under RICO the statute of limitations is four years. The clock starts ticking NOT when the chain of theft began. NOT when the chain of theft ended. **The Statute of Limitations begins when**

victims finally RECOGNIZE that a crime has taken place. Under Civil RICO you are authorized to act as a citizen prosecutor.

Both criminal and civil RICO takes into account that it takes time for victims to recognize how they were harmed by the organized criminal enterprise. Since as they say, "it takes a village," this very organized and predictable chain of theft is described in my book as the Bank Theft Delivery System.

Theft of private property, feeding product to the securities industry is so lucrative that foreign entities have entered this theft market. Undermining private property rights in America with almost no push back from federal law enforcement is a globalist agenda. The S.W.I.F.T System (SCRL) otherwise known as: **Society for Worldwide Interbank Financial Telecommunication** uses a number system to track and facilitate money transfers world-wide. How much American land has China and Mexican drug cartels purchased in this country? Using Mexican drug cartels China has dumped massive amounts of Fentanyl and Meth laced with Fentanyl into this country. Homes acquired by title theft and located in residential neighborhoods could operate as a base and, or, as a safe house. In the national interest these links need to be explored.

CHAPTER TWENTY-FOUR
Dress Up and Show Up.

If you are ambushed to show up in court by all means, smile and show up. This is a good day and should be seen as a prized opportunity not to be squandered. This is your chance to ask for and if necessary, demand documentation, names, dates and particulars that you do not currently have. There will be a court reporter clicking away. Speak to this record. Say what you know so far regarding any possible chain of theft and what you need time (a postponement) to investigate.

In many cases the fraudsters believe you have been so bullied, shamed, and manipulated by their treatment that you will not show up. As common practice the fraudsters may have even interfered with proper notice which will invalidate any decision that you were not present for. This is a violation of your **Procedural Due Process** rights. Lack of notice invalidates the jurisdiction of any court to produce a ruling. Read the 35 Lewis Fairway Circle example in my book; Part Three chapter twenty-six; *Illegal Foreclosure, Title Theft, and its Chain of Corruption.*

1. Ask the judge to grant a six-month delay.
2. Time to find an attorney well versed in Title Theft Schemes; described by the FBI as among the fastest growing crimes in America.

3. State that you have reason to suspect title theft.
4. You have reason to suspect document fraud.
5. You have reason to suspect identity theft.
6. You have reason to suspect some adaptation of a Property Flip – Equity Skimming – Title Theft Scheme.
7. You suspect broken chain of title. Ask the judge to direct the opposing party to produce a complete chain of property title. Doing so by a specific date set by the court. No clean and complete chain of property title free of fraud, doubt, error, and forgery equates to no authority to perfect what contrives to be theft of private property absent due process.
8. Ask the judge to direct the other side to produce by a specific date the complete MERS history of secret transactions by which Property Flip – Equity Skimming – Title Theft Schemes and Mortgage Fraud operate undetected. Quote if need be from chapter nineteen of my book.
9. Do not leave court without having verified and gotten on record the name of the actual party bringing the lawsuit. The first answer will usually be a lie framed in deceptive language. Say so. Ask the judge to verify: **"is that a true and complete answer?"**
10. Read up on the Fourth and Fourteenth Amendments to the U.S. Constitution. The Fourth Amendment guards against illegal search and seizure of your home. Understand your due process rights. Read the description of Procedural

Due Process at the start of this book. Be watchful for those government employees that stand in the way of you discovering the truth you are legally entitled to.

A judgment or decree is invalid where it has no foundation of procedural due process. As where there is an absence of notice or opportunity to be heard. 16A C.J.S. Constitutional Law, § 625; Yellowstone Pipe Line company v. Drummond, 77 Idaho 36, 287 P.2d 288.

CHAPTER TWENTY-FIVE
Fraud is the Fly in the Ointment

Even if you were behind on your house payments, but fraud was involved in the seizure of your home, that would be a void judgment. **Rick A. Slorp vs. Bank of America, N.A; Mortgage Electronic Registration System, Inc.** is just one such case. It was heard on appeal from the lower court. It reads in part: *"The key element here is that the Court's determination that the lawyers were misleading the court by characterizing the homeowner's claim as seeking damages <u>for a false assignment.</u> The Sixth Circuit correctly analyzed the situation and arrived at the simple conclusion: if BOA (Bank of America) didn't have the right to foreclose the mortgage then it doesn't matter whether or not the homeowner defaulted."*

Fraud invalidates everything it enters into. The case reads: *"During the foreclosure case, judgment had been taken against the homeowner without him realizing the problematic documents."*

False Assignment refers to the Breeder Document, Assignment of the Deed of Trust. Go back and read about the three breeder documents and how they drive forward the chain of theft.

An article by reporter Barry Fagan reads: *The district court judge initially dismissed the lawsuit, but today's landmark decision by the federal court of appeals reinstated the most serious of the allegations.* Namely, document fraud. False assignments feature in every example of Title Theft.

As already stated, and cannot be stated enough, in a mortgage and title theft scheme MERS is the identity theft depository. Mortgage Electronic Registration System, Inc., MERSCorp Holding, Inc., collectively known as MERS was among the defendants sued in the Rick A. Slorp Case.

The fraudsters had concealed and failed to file where they could be found the Assignments; transfers of ownership. The Assignment of the Deed of Trust was not recognized by Mr. Slorp as an identity theft breeder document. I made the same mistake. As I tracked the various assignments of my property title and mortgage I found other secret assignments. We tend to trust what we read and especially if that paper appears as properly signed and notarized endorsements. It is perhaps the case that there were other Assignments flowing back and forth amongst the fraud partners putting distance between Mr. Slorp's original deed of trust and the first assignment of the mortgage to criminals.

CHAPTER TWENTY-SIX
CONCLUSION

A void judgment is a nullity, and no rights can be based thereon; <u>it can be set aside on motion or can be collaterally attacked at any time.</u> Garren v. Rollis 375 P.2d 994 (Idaho 1962). Courts lose jurisdiction if they do not follow Due Process Law. Title 5, US Cod Sec. 556(d), Sec. 557, Sec. 706.

A void judgment under federal law is one in which rendering court lacked subject matter jurisdiction over dispute or jurisdiction over the parties, <u>or acted in a manner inconsistent with due process of law or otherwise acted unconstitutionally in entering a judgment.</u> U.S.C.A Const. Amed. 5, Hays v. Louisiana Dock Co., 452 n.e. 2D 1383 (Ill. App.5 Dist. 2983).

"No provision of the Constitution is designed to be without effect;" "Anything that is in conflict is null and void of law;" "Cleary, for a secondary law to come in conflict with the supreme Law was illogical, for certainly the supreme Law would prevail over all other laws and certainly our forefathers had intended that the supreme Law would be the basis of all law and for any law to come in conflict would be null and void of law, it would bare no power to enforce... for unconstitutionality... It operates a near nullity or a fiction of law. Marbury v. Madison: 5 US 137 (1803).

NOTES

Made in the USA
Monee, IL
23 June 2023